ANIMAL SAFARI

Meerkats

by Kari Schuetz

BELLWETHER MEDIA • MINNEAPOLIS, MN

Note to Librarians, Teachers, and Parents:

Blastoff! Readers are carefully developed by literacy experts and combine standards-based content with developmentally appropriate text.

Level 1 provides the most support through repetition of high-frequency words, light text, predictable sentence patterns, and strong visual support.

Level 2 offers early readers a bit more challenge through varied simple sentences, increased text load, and less repetition of high-frequency words.

Level 3 advances early-fluent readers toward fluency through increased text and concept load, less reliance on visuals, longer sentences, and more literary language.

Level 4 builds reading stamina by providing more text per page, increased use of punctuation, greater variation in sentence patterns, and increasingly challenging vocabulary.

Level 5 encourages children to move from "learning to read" to "reading to learn" by providing even more text, varied writing styles, and less familiar topics.

Whichever book is right for your reader, Blastoff! Readers are the perfect books to build confidence and encourage a love of reading that will last a lifetime!

This edition first published in 2012 by Bellwether Media, Inc.

No part of this publication may be reproduced in whole or in part without written permission of the publisher. For information regarding permission, write to Bellwether Media, Inc., Attention: Permissions Department, 5357 Penn Avenue South, Minneapolis, MN 55419.

Library of Congress Cataloging-in-Publication Data

Schuetz, Kari.
  Meerkats / by Kari Schuetz.
      p. cm. – (Blastoff! readers. Animal safari)
  Includes bibliographical references and index.
  Summary: "Developed by literacy experts for students in kindergarten through grade three, this book introduces meerkats to young readers through leveled text and related photos"–Provided by publisher.
  ISBN 978-1-60014-718-0 (hardcover : alk. paper)
  1. Meerkat–Juvenile literature. I. Title.
  QL737.C235S38 2012
  599.74'2–dc23   2011031237

Printed in the United States of America, North Mankato, MN.

010112   1207

Contents

What Are Meerkats?

Meerkats are small **mammals**. They have black circles around their eyes.

Meerkats scurry across grasslands and deserts. They often stand on their back legs.

Meerkats **forage** for food during the day. They eat scorpions, **insects**, and bird eggs.

Meerkats live in **burrows**. These are tunnels they dig underground.

Mobs

Meerkats live in groups called **mobs**. One mob can have 40 meerkats.

Meerkats in
a mob work
together to care
for their young.

Staying Safe

The meerkats also
work as a team
to stay safe.
They take turns
as the **sentry**.

The sentry watches for hawks, hyenas, and other **predators**. It also looks for other mobs.

The sentry barks when it spots danger. This warns other meerkats to run into **bolt holes**. Take cover!

bolt hole

Glossary

bolt holes—escape holes that meerkats dig in the ground; meerkats run into bolt holes when in danger.

burrows—holes or tunnels in the ground where some animals live

forage—to wander in search of food

insects—animals with six legs and hard outer bodies; insect bodies are divided into three parts.

mammals—warm-blooded animals that have backbones and feed their young milk

mobs—groups of meerkats that live together

predators—animals that hunt other animals for food

sentry—a meerkat that stands guard; a sentry barks to warn other meerkats of danger.

To Learn More

AT THE LIBRARY

Clark, Willow. *Meerkats: Life in the Mob.* New York, N.Y.: PowerKids Press, 2011.

Gravett, Emily. *Meerkat Mail.* New York, N.Y.: Simon & Schuster Books for Young Readers, 2007.

Jones, Allan Frewin. *Meerkat in Trouble.* London, U.K.: Happy Cat Books, 2008.

ON THE WEB

Learning more about meerkats is as easy as 1, 2, 3.

1. Go to www.factsurfer.com.

2. Enter "meerkats" into the search box.

3. Click the "Surf" button and you will see a list of related Web sites.

With factsurfer.com, finding more information is just a click away.

Index

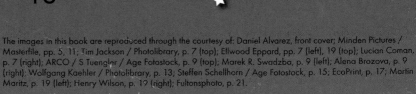

The images in this book are reproduced through the courtesy of: Daniel Alvarez, front cover; Minden Pictures / Masterfile, pp. 5, 11; Tim Jackson / Photolibrary, p. 7 (top); Ellwood Eppard, pp. 7 (left), 19 (top); Lucian Coman, p. 7 (right); ARCO / S Tuengler / Age Fotostock, p. 9 (top); Marek R. Swadzba, p. 9 (left); Alena Brozova, p. 9 (right); Wolfgang Kaehler / Photolibrary, p. 13; Steffen Schellhorn / Age Fotostock, p. 15; EcoPrint, p. 17; Martin Maritz, p. 19 (left); Henry Wilson, p. 19 (right); Fultonsphoto, p. 21.